TABLE OF CONTENTS

INTRODUCTION

On May 11, 2004, the American citizens watching the evening news were introduced

to a new face of terror. The lead news story required broadcasters to warn viewers of the graphic

nature of the video clip that followed. As the video played, one could distinguish an average

looking white male in orange prison garb with his feet bound and knees bent in the foreground.

Five masked men clad in black stood behind him. The prisoner sat motionless while one of the

masked men read a prepared statement in Arabic. The news commentator's voice articulated the

story since a translation of the masked man's words was not yet available. The masked man,

wielding a sword, threw the prisoner to the ground, and America and the world bore witness to

the last moments of American contractor Nicholas Berg's life. His masked executioner was

alleged to be Abu Musab al-Zarqawi. The news real cut the tape just before the knife entered his

neck, yet not before an audible cry was heard from Berg's mouth. Zarqawi's name was faintly

familiar to some who followed the U.S. government's pre-Iraq invasion narrative. His name was

first mentioned by Secretary of State Colin Powell in his address to the United Nations in 2003.

Powell alleged Zarqawi was the key Al Qaeda operative linked to the regime of Sadaam Hussein

as a justification for a pre-emptive strike against the Iraq regime; an assertion later disproven.[1]

This was not the last time the Internet and media savvy public would witness artifacts

from Zarqawi's campaign of terror. Between 2004 and 2006, Zarqawi's network posted countless

videos of suicide bombings, IED attacks, and executions for the world to witness. Citizens read of

the U.S. soldier and civilian deaths attributed to Zarqawi on a seemingly daily basis. Countless

Iraqi and international civilians died by his hands both in Iraq and abroad. Zarqawi was lauded by

---

[1] Colin Powell, *"A Policy of Evasion and Deception: Full Text of U.S. Secretary of State Colin Powell's Speech to the United Nations On Iraq,"* Washington Post Online, http://www.washingtonpost.com/wp-srv/nation/transcripts/powelltext_020503.html (accessed February 7, 2013).

the renowned al Qaeda leader Osama Bin Laden as a lion and the legitimate leader of al Qaeda in Iraq.[2] Sunni extremists and insurgents within Iraq embraced him. He built suicide bomber legions comprised of recruits from as far away as Europe. His name appeared prominently in President Bush's 2006 state of the Union address along with Osama Bin Laden.[3]

Who was Zarqawi and how did this Jordanian juvenile delinquent[4] grow up to become the feared leader of Al Qaeda in Iraq? How did Zarqawi come to warrant a $25 million bounty[5] as the most wanted fugitive in Iraq?[6] This monograph leaves these questions to future historical works. This monograph will instead examine the strategic context and tactical actions surrounding Zarqawi from 2004 to 2006 and the method Zarqawi employed to orchestrate his campaign. The examination seeks to determine if Zarqawi's notorious successes resulted from his employment of a form of operational art against the United States, Iraqi citizens, coalition partners, and the international community from 2004 to 2006. This monograph will examine the strategic, operational, and tactical influences on Zarqawi's organization, planning, and tactics. The methodology will examine the evolution and interrelationships surrounding Al Qaeda in Iraq utilizing Gaddis's scalable lens in order to view the complete landscape in context.[7]

---

[2] Karen DeYoung, "Bin Laden Lauds Al-Zarqawi On Tape / Iraq Al Qaeda Leader, Killed in Bombing, Called 'Lion of Jihad'" *Washington Post,* June 30, 2006.

[3] Sheldon Alberts, "Bush Warns Against Culture of 'defeatism': War On Terror, Iran Top List in Annual Address," *Ottawa Citizen,* 1 February 2006.

[4] Tom Bell, "The Making of a Killer: Radical Islam Helped Turn a Two-Bit Thug Into Terrorist Commanding Global Attention," *Salina Journal,* 15 June 2006.

[5] Claude Salhini, "Method of Zarqawi Madness," *Washington Times*, 30 January 2005.

[6] Loretta Napoleoni, "Profile of a Killer," *Foreign Policy*, 151 (Nov/Dec 2005): 42.

[7] John Lewis Gaddis, *The Landscape of History: How Historians Map the Past* (New York: Oxford University Press, USA, 2004), 4-5.

Both primary and secondary sources relating to Al Qaeda, Bin Laden, Al Qaeda in Iraq, and Zarqawi were used to build this monograph. The recently translated Abbott Abad documents captured in the Bin Laden raid available at The Combatting Terrorism Online Repository provided useful insights to the tensions between Bin Laden and Zarqawi. Congressional Research Reports, thesis, journal articles, newsprint stories and published books provided detailed descriptions of both Al Qaeda and Al Qaeda in Iraq operations and narratives. U.S. military doctrine and military theorists provided the depth and context to derive the definition of operational art as employed in irregular warfare. Future research into the realm of Bin Laden, Al Qaeda, Zarqawi, and Al Qaeda in Iraq will benefit from availability of currently classified primary source documents.

Zarqawi planned and executed operations within the realm of irregular warfare. His story began in a neighborhood in Jordan and reached its crescendo in Iraq from 2004 to 2006. Zarqawi grew from a mere juvenile delinquent to a powerful terrorist cell leader dominating the Iraq threat matrix.[8] This monograph will utilize a derived definition of operational art within irregular warfare and characteristics to determine if Zarqawi employed operational art to contrast with the U.S. Army's understanding. The influence and narrative of al Qaeda will define the strategic context. The history of Zarqawi and his ideology will define the operational context. Discrete examples of Zarqawi's tactical actions in time, space, and purpose compared to characteristics of operational art in irregular warfare will enable a determination of his operational artistry.

The U.S. Army definition of operational art along with its associated elements focuses its applicability on combined arms maneuver and wide area security within the domain of

---

[8] Youssef Aboul-Enein, "Abu Musab Al-Zarqawi an Examination of the Writings of Investigative Journalist Gamal Rahim," *Infantry Magazine*, 98 no. 4 (August-December 2009): 12.

3

conventional nation-state directed warfare.[9] The employment of operational art in the planning and conduct of irregular warfare is not formally defined or addressed in either Army or Joint doctrine. Irregular warfare, by definition, resides in the domain of special or unconventional warfare. Therefore, a derived definition and applicable characteristics of operational art are required in order to determine if an irregular warfare actor, such as Zarqawi, employed operational art in either planning or practice.

Joint Publication 1-02 defines irregular warfare as "a violent struggle among state and non-state actors for legitimacy and influence over the relevant population (s)."[10] The U.S. Army Counterinsurgency Field Manual narrows the Army's irregular warfare definition by describing the spectrum of irregular warfare as existing across a "broad form of conflicts in which insurgency, counterinsurgency, and unconventional warfare are the principle activities."[11] The irregular warfare focus for this monograph is the employment of violent force between a state and non-state actor. The non-state actor for this monograph is a terrorist, insurgent, or member of terror cell or insurgent cause.

U.S. Joint and Army doctrine pose two varying definitions of operational art. Joint Doctrine defines operational art as "the cognitive approach by commanders and staffs – supported by their skill, knowledge, experience, creativity, and judgment – to develop strategies, campaigns, and operations to organize and employ military forces by integrating ends, ways, and means."[12]

---

[9] U.S. Department of the Army, *ADRP 3-0, Unified Land Operations* (Washington, DC, Government Printing Office, May 2012), 4-1.

[10] U.S. Department of Defense, JP 1-02, *Department of Defense Dictionary of Military and Associated Terms* (Washington, DC, Government Printing Office, November 2010), 162.

[11] U.S. Department of the Army, FM 3-24.2, *Tactics in Counterinsurgency* (Washington, DC, Government Printing Office, April 2009), Glossary-12.

[12] U.S. Department of Defense, JP 1-02, *Department of Defense Dictionary of Military and Associated Terms* (Washington, DC, Government Printing Office, November 2010), 216.

The U.S. Army defines operational art as "the pursuit of strategic objectives, in whole or in part, through the arrangement of tactical actions in time, space, and purpose."[13] A definition of operational art in irregular warfare must take into account the unique nature of irregular warfare to include the ideological undertone and unconventional methods as well as key elements within the Joint and Army definitions. Therefore, the proposed definition of operational art for irregular warfare is: *the pursuit of an ideological purpose through the employment of distributed attacks against a superior force and its interests in order to protract the conflict resulting in the decay of that force's support system through denial of rapid achievement of its strategic aim.*

Dr. James Schneider identified eight characteristics of operational art through historical analysis of American Civil War maneuvers.[14] Four of Schneider's operational art characteristics are applicable within the irregular warfare domain. The first characteristic of operational art Schneider addressed is the distributed operation.[15] A distributed operation consists of battles executed in geographical depth yet linked operationally through time under a single purpose.[16] An example of a terrorist based distributed operation occurred in Algeria in 2007 when a group newly aligned with Al Qaeda successfully executed coordinated yet distributed attacks against six police stations and a convoy of oil workers.[17] The second key characteristic of operational art as

---

[13] U.S. Department of the Army, ADRP 3-0, *Unified Land Operations* (Washington, DC, Government Printing Office, May 2012), 4-1.

[14] Schneider, James J., Vulcan's Anvil: The American Civil War and the Foundation of the Operational Art. Theoretical Paper No. 4 (Fort Leavenworth, KS: U.S. Army Command and General Staff College, 2004), 16-17.

[15] Ibid., 35.

[16] Schneider, James J., Vulcan's Anvil: The American Civil War and the Foundation of the Operational Art. Theoretical Paper No. 4 (Fort Leavenworth, KS: U.S. Army Command and General Staff College, 2004), 35.

[17] Craig Smith, "At Least 23 Die in 2 Terrorist Bombings in Algeria," *New York Times*, April 11, 2007.

defined by Schneider is the concept of continuous logistics.[18] The logistical requirements for a terrorist organization operating within a geographic area consist of sustenance, weapon systems, ammunition or explosives, basing, and transportation. Terrorist or irregular forces require a smaller quantity of sustainment than the forces of a field Army. The smaller logistics footprint reduces the required footprint and assets required to maintain lines of communication and operations enhancing the ability of the cell to blend into the environment. The third key characteristic of operational art Schneider highlights is that of an operationally durable formation.[19] The durable formation is designed to conduct distributed operations over an indefinite period of time.[20] The reduced logistical footprint allows durability through lessened exposure to detection and destruction. The final key characteristic of operational art as described by Schneider is the concept of employing operational art against a distributed enemy.[21] In conflicts since September 11, 2001, the U.S. and coalition partners routinely operated from forward operating bases distributed throughout the theaters of operation. Similarly, the new Iraq security forces were distributed adjacent to U.S. bases. Both offered distributed targets for terrorist organizations such as Al Qaeda in Iraq.

Dr. Richard Swain observed another characteristic of operational art applicable to irregular warfare in his analysis of the evolution of U.S. doctrine.[22] Swain noted the July 1986

---

[18] Schneider, James J., Vulcan's Anvil: The American Civil War and the Foundation of the Operational Art. Theoretical Paper No. 4 (Fort Leavenworth, KS: U.S. Army Command and General Staff College, 2004), 41.

[19] Ibid., 50.

[20] Ibid., 50.

[21] Schneider, James J., Vulcan's Anvil: The American Civil War and the Foundation of the Operational Art. Theoretical Paper No. 4 (Fort Leavenworth, KS: U.S. Army Command and General Staff College, 2004), 56.

[22] Richard Swain, ed., "Filling the Void: The Operational Art and the U.S. Army," in The

version of FM 100-5, Operations, stated that operational art "thus involves fundamental decisions about when and where to fight and whether to accept or decline battle. Its essence is the identification of the enemy's operational center of gravity and the employment of superior combat power against that point to achieve a decisive success."[23] Relevant tenets of the 1986 U.S. operational art definition also specify a military force may decide when and where to fight, whether to accept or decline battle, and ultimately identify and target the enemy's center of gravity. An irregular force is not equipped or structured to employ superior combat power against a modern military's in order to achieve a decisive success. When facing a superior military force, an irregular warfare-based organization may face numerous tactical defeats. However, Clausewitz observed that defeat in war is only transient and the irregular warfare force usually decides when and where to fight.[24] Therefore, accepting or declining battle and identifying and targeting the enemy center of gravity are applicable to the irregular warrior, especially if the identified center of gravity is the popular support required of a civilian populous for a protracted conflict. Furthermore, a tactical defeat against a terrorist entity does not translate to defeat of a terrorist organization, as evidenced by the Global War on Terror carried out by the United States. Thus, two additional characteristics of operational art applicable to an irregular force include accepting or denying battle and its ability to target an enemy's center of gravity.

The operational art definition and characteristics serve as the basis to determining if Zarqawi employed operational art. The applicable operational art characteristics derived from doctrine and operational art theorists applicable to the artist practicing irregular warfare are: the

Operational Art: Developments in the Theories of War, ed. B. J. C. McKercher and Michael A. Hennessy (Westport, Conn.: Praeger, 1996), 147-66.

[23] Ibid., 165.

[24] Carl von Clausewitz, *On War*, Indexed Edition, Reprint ed. (Princeton: Princeton University Press, 1989), 80.

employment of distributed operations against a single aim, supporting operations through continuous and distributed logistics, task organize into operationally durable formations, employ operational art against a distributed enemy, choosing to accept or decline battle, and attack an enemy center of gravity.

This monograph utilizes the derived operational art definition and characteristics in irregular warfare to determine if Zarqawi was an operational artist. The monograph is organized to flow from the strategic to the tactical level in order to provide a full context of Zarqawi's operational environment and influences. The first section will describe the strategic organization of Al Qaeda and the strategic narratives of the key leaders Osama Bin Laden and Dr. Ayman al-Zawahiri. The next section will describe Zarqawi's personal journey from the streets of Jordan to leader of Al Qaeda in Iraq. The third section will outline the narrative and organization of Al Qaeda in Iraq. The fourth section will use the derived definition and characteristics of operational art in irregular warfare to analyze Zarqawi's plans and actions from 2004 to 2006. Finally, the monograph concludes Zarqawi did indeed employ a form of operational art against U.S. and coalition forces in Iraq from 2004 to 2006 and the future ramifications of such a determination.

AL QAEDA CENTRAL – THE STRATEGIST

Al Qaeda was formed in 1988 by Osama Bin Laden and a close group of like-minded militants near the end of the mujahedeen fight against Soviet forces in Afghanistan.[25] Bin Laden desired to violently overthrow pro-Western governments in Muslim lands by exporting Al Qaeda fighters and activists to targeted countries.[26] Following the Soviet withdrawal from Afghanistan,

---

[25] Donald Shaffer, "Unraveling Al Qaeda's Strategy" (master's thesis, Joint Advanced Warfighting School, 2005), 10.

[26] U.S. Congressional Research Service, *Al Qaeda: Profile and Threat Assessment,* by Kenneth Katzman, CRS Report for Congress, Federation of American Scientists (Washington, DC, 2005), CRS-2.

Bin Laden moved back to his native Saudi Arabia where he continued to manage Al Qaeda's growth and promote his ideology. Following the Iraqi invasion of Kuwait in 1990 and the Sadaam's forces posturing along the Saudi borders, Bin Laden offered to raise an army of mujahedeen fighters to defend the kingdom. Instead, the Saudi royal family authorized a U.S. troop buildup within the kingdom. Bin Laden was furious. The admission of U.S. troops into the kingdom of Saudi Arabia ultimately led to Bin Laden's fallout with the Royal family and added fuel to his jihadist messages of non-Muslims fighting in Muslim lands. Bin Laden left the kingdom following his expulsion and moved to Sudan where he established Al Qaeda headquarters and launched operations in Afghanistan.[27]

Al Qaeda's second in command, Dr. Ayman al-Zawahiri arrived in Afghanistan to join the mujahedeen in 1985 following imprisonment in his native Egypt for accusations of attempting to assassinate Egyptian President Sadat.[28] Zawahiri led a group of fighters known as Al Jihad. As an early indication of what would later become Al Qaeda's strategy for growth, Bin Laden convinced Zawahiri to bring Al Jihad under the Al Qaeda banner.[29] Al Qaeda continued to recruit and train fighters and grow its base of operations in Afghanistan while sheltered by the Taliban regime. In 1996, Bin Laden entered the global stage by officially declaring Jihad against the United States.[30] Bin Laden lamented the United States for occupying Muslim lands in Saudi

---

[27] Peter Bergen, *The Osama Bin Laden I Know: an Oral History of Al Qaeda's Leader* (New York: Free Press, 2006), 115.

[28] U.S. Congressional Research Service, *Al Qaeda: Profile and Threat Assessment,* by Kenneth Katzman, CRS Report for Congress, Federation of American Scientists (Washington, DC, 2005), CRS-2.

[29] Ibid., CRS-7.

[30] U.S. Congressional Research Service, *Al Qaeda: Statements and Evolving Ideology,* by Christopher M. Blanchard, CRS Report for Congress, Congressional Research Service (Washington, DC, 2005), CRS-3.

Arabia in addition to openly supporting Israel.[31] Bin Laden shared Al Qaeda's narrative in a 1997 interview: "Muslims need a leader who can unite them and establish a pious caliphate. The pious caliphate will start from Afghanistan…. Allah's rule will be established."[32] Bin Laden verbally confirmed Al Qaeda's strategy to establish a caliphate and insure Islamic law throughout Muslim lands in subsequent interviews and messages. Kalyvas observed that control over areas and populations enables the shielding of the population from rival narratives while generating loyalty for the controlling faction.[33] Al Qaeda sought to grow through executing tight sharia based control in Afghanistan and slowly expanding control throughout Arab lands and eventually globally – a total caliphate. Bin Laden stated the methods Al Qaeda sought to achieve the caliphate when he issued a fatwa in 1998. The fatwa "legalized" the targeting of U.S. civilians in addition, to U.S. military personnel, by any Muslim.[34] Al Qaeda continued to issue statements and messages urging Muslims to unite in Al Qaeda's cause while continuing to build fighters and strength to export jihad from Afghanistan.

Al Qaeda was linked to numerous attacks against U.S. interests prior to the September 11, 2001 attack. A short list of substantiated attacks by Al Qaeda include the 1993 World Trade Center bombings, 1993 Somali faction attacks against U.S. forces in Mogadishu, the 1995 attempted assassination of Egyptian president Mubarak, the 1995 bombing of a U.S. military

---

[31] U.S. Congressional Research Service, *Al Qaeda: Statements and Evolving Ideology,* by Christopher M. Blanchard, CRS Report for Congress, Congressional Research Service (Washington, DC, 2005), CRS-3.

[32] Hamid Mir, "Pakistan Interviews Usama Bin Laden" (Islamabad, Pakistan 18 March, 1997).

[33] Stathis N. Kalyvas, *The Logic of Violence in Civil War* (New York: Cambridge University Press, 2006), 118-125.

[34] Donald Shaffer, "Unraveling Al Qaeda's Strategy" (master's thesis, Joint Advanced Warfighting School, 2005), 20-21.

advisory facility in Riyadh, the 1996 bombing of the Khobar Towers, the 1998 bombings of the

U.S. embassies in Kenya and Tanzania, and the 2000 bombing of the U.S.S. Cole in Yemen.[35] Al

Qaeda continued to grow in popularity and strength following the success of each attack. Al

Qaeda culminated in spectacular attacks with the September 11, 2001 attacks against the World

Trade Center and the Pentagon. As a result of September 11th, Al Qaeda expanded its strength by

gaining the pledged affiliation of several Jihadist groups from Egypt, Algeria, Uzbekistan, and

Indonesia.[36] Following his dislodgement from Afghanistan in 2001 by U.S. and coalition forces,

Bin Laden retained leadership of Al Qaeda. However, he became dependent on the newly aligned

subordinate cells and organizations to carry out continued tactical attacks under the Al Qaeda

banner the central al Qaeda leadership adjusted to the newly distributed organization.

Prior to fleeing Afghanistan, Al Qaeda had grown into a mature and structured

organization consisting of militant brigades, advisory counsels, and functional committees to

oversee finances, training, security, and information operations.[37] The Shura committee

comprised of Bin Laden and his inner circle of advisors guided the organization.[38] Al Qaeda

recruited thousands of foot soldiers from all countries to attend training camps operated

throughout Afghanistan.[39] In line with Bin Laden's founding ideals, the trained fighters were sent

---

[35] U.S. Congressional Research Service, *Al Qaeda: Profile and Threat Assessment,* by Kenneth Katzman, CRS Report for Congress, Federation of American Scientists (Washington, DC, 2005), CRS-4 – CRS-5.

[36] Ibid., CRS-4 – CRS-8.

[37] Donald Shaffer, "Unraveling Al Qaeda's Strategy" (master's thesis, Joint Advanced Warfighting School, 2005), 12.

[38] Ibid., 12.

[39] Mark E. Stout, Jessica M. Huckabey, and John R. Schindler, *The Terrorist Perspectives Project: Strategic and Operational Views of Al Qaida and Associated Movements* (Annapolis, MD.: Naval Institute Press, 2008), 201.

back to their native countries armed with weapons proficiency, knowledge of military tactics, and bomb making skills to carry out jihad. Training camps were open to all like-minded jihadist fighters regardless of country of origin. Many of the successful attacks previously mentioned and credited to Al Qaeda were not directly planned or executed by central Al Qaeda leadership or even the brigade of fighters. However, many of the attackers and cell leaders were graduates of the Al Qaeda training camps. Bin Laden, in cooperation with the Al Qaeda Emir Shura Advisory Council that consisted of his inner circle, claimed to approve the terrorist strikes under the Al Qaeda name and shared the motives of the tactical actors.[40] The September 11, 2001 attacks were the result of the maturation of the hierarchical and distributed networks of Al Qaeda planning, financing, and execution of a large-scale attack.

Following the invasion of Afghanistan and the loss of Al Qaeda's safe haven, the strategic organization maintained communications through its multi-media arm, al-Sahab. Al-Sahab began production of Al Qaeda's strategic messaging in 2000 and matured into a multi-media production arm distributing sub-titled videos, voice messages, written communication, and even 3-D graphics.[41] Al-Sahab distributed Al Qaeda messages to legitimate media organizations, such as Al Jazeera, in addition to online publishing through various untraceable Internet sites. The surviving members of Al Qaeda's Shura council, to include Bin Laden and Zawahiri, remained loosely in charge of the organization and continued to issue guidance and narratives through al-Sahab. The international efforts to kill and capture key leaders disaggregated the large mature

---

[40] U.S. Congressional Research Service, *Al Qaeda: Statements and Evolving Ideology*, by Christopher M. Blanchard, CRS Report for Congress, Congressional Research Service (Washington, DC, 2005), CRS-4.

[41] Craig Whitlock, "The New Al-Qaeda Central," *Washington Post,* September 9, 2007.

organization over the course of 2002 and 2003. However, what was referred to as Al Qaeda

Central, re-emerged in 2003 with Bin Laden's release of his "Message to the Iraqi People."[42]

The metamorphosed Al Qaeda Central[43] consisted of Bin Laden as the strategic and

idealist leader of the organization with Zawahiri assuming the role of the operations commander.

Other key leaders and trusted associates, to include Adam Gadahn, lead regional-based

subordinate organizations. The popularity of the Al Qaeda name within jihad circles continued to

grow. Groups began pledging allegiance to Bin Laden and Al Qaeda and crediting attacks to its

name.[44] At a minimum, Bin Laden maintained a written correspondence relationship with many

of the affiliate leaders. He rarely publicly acknowledges formal regional affiliations. However,

Zawahiri recognized several groups in messages; although it remains unknown if Bin Laden

concurred in these endorsements. Al Qaeda reaffirmed their strategic narrative when Zawahiri

issued the three foundations of Al Qaeda in 2005 as the creation of Islamic states under sharia

law, liberation of Muslim lands from non-Muslim interference, and governments and people

mutually accountable for Islamic laws and principles.[45] The strategic approach to achieve the

three foundations included the expulsion of U.S. military from Muslim lands, removal of Western

sympathetic governments in the Middle East, creation of sharia law-based Islamic governments, a

---

[42] Peter Bergen, *The Osama Bin Laden I Know: An Oral History of Al Qaeda's Leader* (New York: Free Press, 2006), 351.

[43] Al Qaeda Central is a Western term used to denote the mainstay Al Qaeda organization as controlled by Bin Laden and his close advisors. The term is used to denote the Al Qaeda strategic organization from subsidiaries liberally claiming use of the Al Qaeda name.

[44] Nelly Lahoud et al., "Letters from Abbottabad: Bin Ladin Sidelined?" The Combating Terrorism Center at West Point (3 May 2012): 10, www.ctc.usma.edu

[45] *U.S. Congressional Research Service, Al Qaeda: Statements and Evolving Ideology,* by Christopher M. Blanchard, CRS Report for Congress, Congressional Research Service (Washington, DC, 2005), CRS-9 – CRS-10.

military defeat of Israel, and the conversion of Shiite Muslims to Sunni.[46] This religious tension between the Sunni and Shiite would later powerfully undermine Zarqawi's religious narrative in his terror campaign. Bin Laden drew special attention to Iraq, Somalia, and Afghanistan as the key jihad battlegrounds. He viewed the Iraqi insurgency in 2004 and 2005 as the means to create the capital of the caliphate in Baghdad from where jihad could project. Al Qaeda Central had to rely on regional affiliates and jihadist fighters to execute operational and tactical operations.

Al Qaeda Central retained the approval authority for major attacks. Strategic guidance to regionally based affiliate organizations was issued through written correspondence and al-Sahab Internet messaging.[47] Acquired Al Qaeda affiliates were permitted and encouraged to continue regional actions and maintain autonomy in execution of local tactical attacks.[48] Al Qaeda Central retained approval authority for large-scale operations. Al Qaeda Central's focus remained on growth and expansion to achieve the three foundations Zawahiri laid out in 2005. However, evidence seized in the Abbottabad raid indicated tension between Bin Laden's ideal approach and the regional affiliates' methods of operations.[49]

The U.S. invasion into Iraq in 2003 set the stage for the reemergence of a distributed Al Qaeda Central on the international stage. The United States invasion of a Muslim land in the heart of the Middle East enabled Al Qaeda to shift the strategic narrative to a defensive jihad, which

---

[46] U.S. Congressional Research Service, *Al Qaeda: Statements and Evolving Ideology*, by Christopher M. Blanchard, CRS Report for Congress, Congressional Research Service (Washington, DC, 2005), CRS-14.

[47] Eric Schmitt, "Jet Plot Shows Growing Ability of Qaeda Affiliates," *New York Times*, December 31, 2009.

[48] Leah Farrall, "How Al Qaeda Works: What the Organization's Subsidiaries Say About Its Strength," *Foreign Affairs Journal* 90, no. 2 (Mar/Apr 2011): 128-38.

[49] Nelly Lahoud et al., "Letters from Abbottabad: Bin Ladin Sidelined?" The Combating Terrorism Center at West Point (3 May 2012): 11-12, www.ctc.usma.edu.

increased ideological affiliation. A defensive jihad is invoked when non-Muslims entities invade Muslim lands.[50] Defensive jihad is generally considered a more legitimate ground for holy war.[51] Al Azhar, the university in Cairo dedicated to Islamic studies, as well as the Hezbollah leader Sheikh Fadlallah issued fatwas against the "invaders of Iraq."[52] The independent fatwas emboldened Bin Laden and Zawahiri to dramatically increase strategic messaging in 2004. Al Qaeda began offering rewards and encouragement for the legitimized continued killing of coalition leaders, troops, and Western-cooperating Iraqi government officials. However, Al Qaeda needed a formal regional affiliate in Iraq to carry the operational planning and execution of the cause. The leader, Abu Musab al Zarqawi accepted the Al Qaeda name and pledged allegiance to Bin Laden. Zarqawi is the only Al Qaeda affiliate in Iraq Bin Laden personally and publicly admitted into Al Qaeda.[53]

ABU MUSAB AL-ZARQAWI – THE ARTIST

Zarqawi, Born Ahmad Fadil Nazzal Al-Khalayleh on October 20, 1966 in Zarqa, Jordan, was raised in a middle class family whose tribe was loyal to the monarch based on his father's public service employment.[54] Zarqawi was scholastically a below average student yet he excelled at art and sports.[55] Following a life a petty crime and job losses, Zarqawi studied the radical

---

[50] Peter Bergen, *The Osama Bin Laden I Know: an Oral History of Al Qaeda's Leader* (New York: Free Press, 2006), 350.

[51] Ibid., 350.

[52] Ibid., 350-351.

[53] Nelly Lahoud et al., "Letters from Abbottabad: Bin Ladin Sidelined?" The Combating Terrorism Center at West Point (3 May 2012): 10, www.ctc.usma.edu.

[54] Jean-Charles Brisard with Damien Martinez, *Zarqawi: the New Face of Al-Qaeda* (New York: Other Press, 2005), 10-11.

[55] Ibid., 11.

Islamic teachings of Syyid Qutb prior to leaving home for jihadist exploits in Afghanistan in 1989.[56] Qutb's work, which also influenced Al Qaeda Central, called for a return to Sharia law and the establishment of a true Muslim world free of any and all Western and modern influences.[57] In Afghanistan, Zarqawi received weapons and explosives training. He worked with Saleh al-Hami. Al-Hami worked for Abudullah Azzaman, the spiritual leader of al-Qaeda, and published the magazine *Al-Jihad*.[58] Though Zarqawi was not formally a member of Al Qaeda, he associated with many of the organizations senior members.

Zarqawi returned to Jordan from Afghanistan in 1994 and formed a militant cell with fellow Qutb follower Abu Muhammad al-Madisi.[59] The cell, known as Bayt Al-Imam, was funded by Bin Laden and armed with Iraqi munitions purchased by al-Madisi on the Kuwaiti black market.[60] Zarqawi and al-Madisi were arrested and charged with possessions of bombs, mines, and illegal passports and were incarcerated in Jordanian prisons.[61] Throughout his prison sentence, Zarqawi rose in power among prisoners. He evolved his ideology to fight all unbelievers, or anyone not a practicing Salafist Sunni Muslim.[62] Zarqawi was released from

---

[56] Youssef Aboul-Enein, "Abu Musab Al-Zarqawi an Examination of the Writings of Investigative Journalist Gamal Rahim," *Infantry Magazine* 98, no. 4 (August-December 2009): 12.

[57] Paul Berman, "The Philosopher of Islamic Terror," *New York Times Magazine*, March 2003.

[58] Youssef Aboul-Enein, "Abu Musab Al-Zarqawi an Examination of the Writings of Investigative Journalist Gamal Rahim," *Infantry Magazine* 98, no. 4 (August-December 2009): 12.

[59] Ibid., 13.

[60] Jean-Charles Brisard with Damien Martinez, *Zarqawi: the New Face of Al-Qaeda* (New York: Other Press, 2005), 35-37.

[61] Ibid., 41.

[62] Ibid., 42-51.

prison under a general amnesty program when King Abdullah took the throne in 1999.[63] The

results of Zarqawi's prison education included increased physical strength and stature,

development as a leader, refined organizational and recruiting skills, and externalization of his

extremist philosophy.[64] He also developed strong relationships with future members and

influencers of Al-Qaeda in Iraq.[65]

Following his reluctant release from prison, Zarqawi departed Jordan for Pakistan

where he was arrested and released and subsequently relocated back to Afghanistan. He

established a terrorist training facility in Herat with assistance from his former mujahedeen

associates.[66] He developed a network of contacts within Al Qaeda as well as other terrorist

organizations. Zarqawi built his terrorist cell with funding assistance from Al Qaeda and began to

grow his group with like-minded Jordanians.[67] During this period, Zarqawi also developed

contacts in Iraq Kurdistan in order to incite attacks on both Jordan and the Democratic Party of

Kurdistan under the banner of Ansar Al-Islam.[68] Zarqawi remained intent on terrorizing the

Western sympathetic government of Jordan. Zarqawi now had connections with key Al Qaeda

figures, his cell in northern Iraq, and a large network of associates and sympathizers. There are

conflicting accounts of Zarqawi's actions and whereabouts between September 11, 2001 and his

---

[63] Youssef Aboul-Enein, "Abu Musab Al-Zarqawi an Examination of the Writings of Investigative Journalist Gamal Rahim," *Infantry Magazine* 98, no. 4 (August-December 2009): 13.

[64] Randy Schliep, "A Time to Kill: When Is Leadership Targeting an Effective Counterterrorism Strategy" (master's thesis, Naval Postgraduate School, 2007), 42.

[65] Ibid., 43.

[66] Jean-Charles Brisard with Damien Martinez, *Zarqawi: the New Face of Al-Qaeda* (New York: Other Press, 2005), 64-70.

[67] Ibid., 74.

[68]Ibid., 78-79.

reemergence in Iraq in 2003. However, he did infiltrate Northern Iraqi-Kurdistan with the

assistance of Ansar al-Islam and formed the group al-Taweed wal Jihad in April 2003.[69]

The United States identified Zarqawi as a leader and member of Al Qaeda when Colin

Powell addressed the United Nations in February 2003.[70] However, the official merger of

Zarqawi's Iraqi terrorist network and Al Qaeda Central would not occur until 2004 as a result of

the U.S. invasion of Iraq. Zarqawi had to this point resisted a formal alliance with Bin Laden.

Zarqawi was in Iraq as early as 2002 working with Ansar al-Islam to build fighter camps and

stockpile weapons for the training and employment of fighters.[71] However, he was not a formal

Al Qaeda affiliate colluding with the Baathist regime. Ansar al Islam dispersed following a U.S.

led bombing effort and direct action attacks by Special Operations Forces in northern Iraq.

Zarqawi had already planned and executed several key attacks under the banner of Ansar al

Islam. According to the Department of State, Ansar al Islam was responsible for the attempted

bombings of the millennium celebration in Jordan in December 1999 and the 2002 assassination

of U.S. diplomat John Foley in Jordan.[72] Following the U.S. invasion of Iraq, the opportunity

emerged to engage the far enemy and the near enemy simultaneously. Zarqawi finally pledged an

oath to Bin Laden in October 2004 and changed the name of *al-Taweed wal Jihad* to *Qa'dat Al-*

Jihad Fi Bilad Al Rifidain or *Al Qaeda in the Land of Two Rivers*, as termed by Western media as

---

[69] Youssef Aboul-Enein, "Abu Musab Al-Zarqawi an Examination of the Writings of Investigative Journalist Gamal Rahim," *Infantry Magazine* 98, no. 4 (August-December 2009): 15.

[70] Steven Weisman, "Threats and Responses: Security Council; Powell, in U.n. Speech, Presents Case to Show Iraq Has Not Disarmed," *New York Times*, February 6, 2003.

[71] Jean-Charles Brisard with Damien Martinez, *Zarqawi: the New Face of Al-Qaeda* (New York: Other Press, 2005), 118-120.

[72] U.S. Congressional Research Service, *Iraq and Al Qaeda,* by Kenneth Katzman, CRS Report for Congress, Congressional Research Service (Washington, DC, 2007), CRS-6.

Al Qaeda in Iraq. While Taweed focused on Jordanian and Israeli targets, the emergent Al-Qaeda in Iraq would shift focus to not only the U.S. and coalition forces, but also all Iraq based non-believers.[73] Zarqawi was in a position to radically execute the basis of his Salafist-Jihadist beliefs by applying the *takfir* (unbeliever) label to not only coalition forces, but also to non-Sunni Muslims, primarily the Shia, assisting the coalition and the Iraqi government.[74]

AL QAEDA IN IRAQ – THE OPERATIONAL ORGANIZATION

The U.S. invasion of Iraq on March 19, 2003 empowered Zarqawi and his Taweed organization through the creation of a previously impossible relationship. Zarqawi had continuously resisted the banner of Al Qaeda based his differences in Salafist-Jihadist ideological beliefs with Bin Laden. Zarqawi maintained that all non-Sunni caliphate-focused Muslims were *takfir* and thus legitimate targets of violence while bin-Laden refused to intentionally target any Muslims. The common interests of Taweed and Al Qaeda came to light as the far enemy of Western Powers entered the Muslim lands of Iraq. Bin Laden had previously funded Zarqawi's training camp in Herat prior to 2001, yet Zarqawi remained independent and refused to swear an oath to the Al Qaeda leader.[75] In 2003, Bin Laden released a statement celebrating the emergent Iraqi insurgents and encouraging young fighters from neighboring countries to join the fight.[76] Bin Laden further issued statements in 2004 offering rewards for the killing of Ambassador

---

[73] Peter Bergen, *The Osama Bin Laden I Know: an Oral History of Al Qaeda's Leader* (New York: Free Press, 2006), 356.

[74] Timothy Kraner, "Al Qaeda in Iraq: Demobilizing the Threat" (master's thesis, Naval Postgraduate School, 2005), 23.

[75] Harmony Project "Cracks in the Foundation: Leadership Schisms in Al Qa'ida1989-2006" The Combating Terrorism Center at West Point (September 2007): 18, www.ctc.usma.edu.

[76] Peter Bergen, *The Osama Bin Laden I Know: an Oral History of Al Qaeda's Leader* (New York: Free Press, 2006), 351.

Bremer and senior coalition leaders in addition to calling fighters to disrupt Iraq's oil industry.[77]

Following Bin Laden's rhetoric encouraging the Iraqi resistance, Zarqawi authored a letter to Bin Laden outlining the enemies of Iraq as the Americans, the Kurds, the Iraqi Security Forces, and the Shia Muslims.[78] It was only a short time later when Zarqawi pledged an oath to Bin Laden and formally created Al Qaeda in Iraq (AQI).

Zarqawi's pledge to Bin Laden under the Al Qaeda banner increased his resources and financing in addition to bolstering recruiting.[79] Zarqawi had already established the legitimacy of his organization through the bombing attacks in Baghdad and Karbala during the Shia festival of Ashura in March of 2004.[80] These attacks were preceded by the bombing of the Jordanian embassy in Baghdad, the vehicle born improvised explosive devise (VBIED) attack on the UN Headquarters in Baghdad, and the VBIED attack at the Imam Ali Mosque in 2003.[81] While Bin Laden sought to capitalize on Al Qaeda's defensive jihad against the far, now near enemy, Zarqawi continued to focus his efforts against Shia targets in order to incite sectarian violence. Zarqawi's strategy was ultimately to create a full Iraqi civil war where the Sunni minority would defeat the Shia, while the U.S. and coalition forces were bled of popular support on the home front.[82] The ultimate withdrawal of coalition forces and the victorious Sunni could

---

[77] Peter Bergen, *The Osama Bin Laden I Know: an Oral History of Al Qaeda's Leader* (New York: Free Press, 2006), 352.

[78] Ibid., 362-363.

[79] Fawaz A. Gerges, *The Far Enemy: Why Jihad Went Global* (New York: Cambridge University Press, 2005), 258.

[80] U.S. Department of State, Office or the Coordinator for Counterterrorism, Country Reports on Terrorism 2005, open-file report, (Washington, DC, 2006), 219-20.

[81] Ibid., 219-20.

[82] U.S. Congressional Research Service, *Iraq and Al Qaeda, by Kenneth Katzman,* CRS Report for Congress, Congressional Research Service (Washington, DC, 2007), CRS-11.

finally establish the capital of the caliphate in Iraq and create the base to spread to neighboring Muslim lands. Bin Laden had sought a leader to regain the Al Qaeda momentum lost following ejection from Afghanistan. He found that leader in Zarqawi.

Zarqawi, under Al Qaeda in Iraq orchestrated a campaign of terror to attain his operational goals. Estimates indicate Al Qaeda in Iraq was responsible for over 700 suicide bombings in Iraq alone.[83] Zarqawi exploited successful attacks with a propaganda-infused messaging campaign. Al Qaeda in Iraq posted and produced videos of attacks. The most notable videos were the beheadings of American contractors Nick Berg and Eugene Armstrong. Zarqawi released edited videos with music and logos detailing multiple suicide bombings against coalition targets interspersed with AQI messages and clips of Bin Laden.[84] Zarqawi even named a chief of media operations for AQI.[85] The propaganda campaign both increased AQI's name recognition and bolstered recruiting. Zarqawi posted narratives and messages in web-based releases to include video taped statements from suicide bombers following their successful strikes. Zarqawi praised fellow insurgent attacks and successes in video and audio clips. He consistently ensured that all messages praised Allah and included religious based justifications for Al Qaeda in Iraq's attacks.

The active membership of AQI between 2004 and 2006 is unknown. State Department estimates AQI consisted of approximately 1000 active members in 2005 [86] while other estimates

---

[83] Peter Bergen and Paul Cruickshank, "Self-Fulfilling Prophecy," *Mother Jones* 32, no. 6 (Nov/Dec 2007): 49.

[84] Associated Press, "Al-Zarqawi Purportedly Releases Propaganda Video", *USA Today*, 7/1/2005.

[85] Timothy Kraner, "Al Qaeda in Iraq: Demobilizing the Threat" (master's thesis, Naval Postgraduate School, 2005), 18.

[86] U.S. United States Department of State, Office or the Coordinator for Counterterrorism, Country Reports on Terrorism 2005, open-file report, (Washington, DC, 2006),

place the number between 1500 and 5000.[87] The same report in 2006 simply listed AQI

manpower-based strength as the largest terrorist organization operating in Iraq.[88] The general

consensus is that AQI probably operated with less than 2000 core members and made up between

10-12% of the active insurgency, although AQI was recognized as the most violent insurgent

group during this time period.[89] Regardless of strength, the makeup of Taweed in pre-invasion

Northern Iraq was largely Palestinian and Jordanian. Following the transition to AQI,

membership expanded to encompass Iraqis, Saudis, Yemenis, and North Africans.[90] Zarqawi

remained accessible to only his most trusted lieutenants, yet maintained operational control over

attacks. According to a Multi-National Forces-Iraq briefing, AQI operatives were classified into

three tiers. Tier one operatives comprised the key leaders and trustees with direct access to

Zarqawi. Tier two operatives were the regional cell leaders who planned, coordinated, and

enabled attacks within assigned regions. Tier three operatives were the individual cell leaders

responsible for the execution of attacks. Zarqawi stood as the powerful and charismatic leader

maintaining the AQI network while cells and groups maintained autonomy in organization and

---

220.

[87] Youssef Aboul-Enein, "Abu Musab Al-Zarqawi an Examination of the Writings of Investigative Journalist Gamal Rahim," *Infantry Magazine* 98, no. 4 (August-December 2009): 15.

[88] U.S. United States Department of State, Office or the Coordinator for Counterterrorism, Country Reports on Terrorism 2006, open-file report, (Washington, DC, 2007), 272.

[89] Anthony Cordesman, Eric Brewer, and Sara Bjerg, "The Islamists and the Zarqawi Factor," (Washington D.C.: Center for Strategic and International Studies, 2006), 3-4.

[90] Timothy Kraner, "Al Qaeda in Iraq: Demobilizing the Threat" (master's thesis, Naval Postgraduate School, 2005), 27-29.

execution of attacks against assigned targets in order to maintain security.[91] The regional cells executed operations within Zarqawi's operational framework and intent.[92]

Zarqawi's methods were not always welcomed. In an intercepted letter in 2005, Zawahiri rebuked Zarqawi for his attacks on Shias.[93] Zawahiri further advised Zarqawi to cease posting the violent media releases, such as the beheadings, as they were negatively affecting the support base for Al Qaeda.[94] Zarqawi continued to implement Sharia law in AQI controlled territory in Al Anbar, specifically in the town of Qaim.[95] The growing resistance by the Sheiks resulted from strong-handed fear tactics of reprisal by AQI that began to alienate Zarqawi from the Sunni population he relied on for support.[96] Although Zarqawi continued attacks against the Shia, he did attempt to rebrand AQI by forming the Mujahedeen Shura Council in 2006.[97] The council unified several insurgent groups in addition to creating a shadow government equipped with ministers of departments such as education, health, and protection.[98] However, the roots of

---

[91] Anthony Cordesman, *Zarqawi's Death: Temporary "Victory" or Lasting Impact* (Washington D.C.: Center for Strategic and International Studies, 2006), 4.

[92] Randy Schliep, "A Time to Kill: When Is Leadership Targeting an Effective Counterterrorism Strategy" (master's thesis, Naval Postgraduate School, 2007), 73.

[93] Harmony Project "Cracks in the Foundation: Leadership Schisms in Al Qa'ida1989-2006" The Combating Terrorism Center at West Point (September 2007): 20, www.ctc.usma.edu.

[94] Ibid.

[95] Ellen Knickmeyer and Jonathan Finer, "Insurgents Assert Control Over Town Near Syrian Border," *Washington Post*, September 6, 2005.

[96] Ibid.

[97] Sean McClure, "The Lost Caravan: The Rise and Fall of Al Qaeda in Iraq, 2003-2007" (master's thesis, Naval Postgraduate School, 2010), 81.

[98] Ibid., 81.

what would become the Sunni Awakening were beginning to grow out of resentment for AQI's tactics and the lack of Sunni political representation in the new Iraqi government.

Overall, from 2003 to 2006, Al Qaeda in Iraq by most accounts made noticeable progress towards the stated goals of inciting a civil war and bleeding out the coalition forces. AQI was instrumental in bringing out the Shia militias of Muqtada al-Sadr and the Sunni death squads. Steven Biddle pointed out the conflicts between Sunnis and Shias and summarized Iraq was in fact immersed in a Civil War.[99] Furthermore, the 2004 U.S. Presidential election revolved around how to resolve the perceived quagmire in Iraq. Popular support for the war was at an all time low. The anti-war rhetoric emerging from the U.S. population calling for an Iraqi withdrawal was growing stronger.[100] Regardless of the strategic tension between Bin Laden and Zarqawi, AQI was effectively making strides towards the strategic goals of inciting a civil war and expelling the Coalition from lack of popular support back home. Bin Laden envisioned the jihadists' ejection of a weakened United States from Iraq would emotionally empower Muslims to rise up against pro-Western governments without fear of U.S. reprisals.[101] AQI was progressing towards Bin Laden's strategic aim even though Al Qaeda Central frowned upon his operational approach.

AQI, ZARQAWI AND OPERATIONAL ART?

The strategic to tactical link from Al Qaeda central to Al Qaeda in Iraq from 2004 to 2006 did not follow the Western military model of operational art in arranging tactical actions in

---

[99] Stephen Biddle, "Seeing Baghdad, Thinking Saigon," *Foreign Affairs Journal* 85, no. 2 (March/April 2006): 2-14.

[100] Adam Nagourney, "With Election Driven by Iraq, Voters Want New Approach," *New York Times*, November 2, 2006.

[101] Nelly Lahoud et al., "Letters from Abbottabad: Bin Ladin Sidelined?" The Combating Terrorism Center at West Point (3 May 2012): 3, www.ctc.usma.edu.

time, space, and purpose to achieve the strategic aim. However, Zarqawi clearly communicated his operational objectives through media conglomerates. The analysis below compares the actions, plans, and purpose of Al Qaeda in Iraq based on the characteristics of operational art in irregular warfare as described in the first section.

Employment of distributed operations against a single aim

Schneider's distributed operations characteristic described battles spanning across space and time unified under a single aim. A battle for Al Qaeda in Iraq consisted of a single or synchronized attack usually executed through suicide bombers. Zarqawi began his offensive campaign against the Coalition support network in August 2003. Al Qaeda in Iraq first bombed the Jordanian Embassy in Baghdad. The attack was followed twelve days later by the truck bombing of the United Nations headquarters in Baghdad. The United Nations attack killed 23 personnel including the United Nations special Representative for Iraq.[102] Zarqawi also initiated offensive attacks in the same month against the Shia when he targeted the Imam Ali Mosque in al Najaf, which killed 75 worshipers and the leader of the Supreme Council for the Islamic Revolution of Iraq.[103] In line with Zarqawi's strategic aim of creating the caliphate starting with Iraq, he simultaneously opened his operations against coalition forces and the Shia population.[104] He hoped continued operations against the U.S. and Shia would lead to the expulsion of U.S. forces resulting from an uncontrollable a civil war. He envisioned that the Sunni would rise up and expel the Shia from Iraq.

---

[102] U.S. United States Department of State, Office or the Coordinator for Counterterrorism, Country Reports on Terrorism 2006, open-file report, (Washington, DC, 2006), 270.

[103] Ibid., 270.

[104] Loretta Napoleoni, "Profile of a Killer," *Foreign Policy* 151 (Nov/Dec 2005): 42.

Zarqawi's attacks ranged from single suicide bombers to large-scale complex attacks spanning multiple cities. He followed attacks with an internet-based media campaign explaining the intent behind the attacks and encouraging jihadists to join Al Qaeda in Iraq in the fight against the coalition and the Shia. Zarqawi's organization claimed responsibility or was credited with attacks against Shia mosques, markets, and cities to include Kadhimiya, Najaf, Samarra, Howaidar, Baquba, and Shia sections of Baghdad.[105] Zarqawi sought to incite the Shia militias to attack Sunni in retaliation. He rightly believed the Sunni would rise up against the vengeful Shia thus creating ripe conditions for the emergence of civil war. Ideally, he hoped the Sunni would annihilate the Shia population in Iraq. As already mentioned, Zarqawi violently introduced himself to the American public in May 2004 when he recorded the beheading of Nicholas Berg. The beheading video quickly went viral and spread across the Internet thanks to Zarqawi's savvy media operations. Zarqawi followed Berg's execution with the beheading of Americans Jack Armstrong and Jack Hensely in September 2004.[106]

Al Qaeda in Iraq maintained strong Sunni support early in the insurgency. Zarqawi's organization provided trained fighters, funding, and a seemingly endless flow of recruits and sympathizers for the resistance.[107] Zarqawi continued to execute attacks against both coalition and Shia. Upon aligning with Bin Laden, Al Qaeda in Iraq saw an exponential influx of international notoriety, recruiting, and funding. Zarqawi also trained and exported jihadist fighters

---

[105] Raj Purohit and Golzar Kheiltash, "Law and Ethics: Indicting Zarqawi for Genocide," *Georgetown Journal of International Affairs* 7, no. 2 (Summer 2006): 93.

[106] U.S. United States Department of State, Office or the Coordinator for Counterterrorism, Country Reports on Terrorism 2006, open-file report, (Washington, DC, 2006), 270.

[107] Sean McClure, "The Lost Caravan: The Rise and Fall of Al Qaeda in Iraq, 2003-2007" (master's thesis, Naval Postgraduate School, 2010), 64.

back to their home countries to await orders. Zarqawi was setting the stage to launch AQI internationally following success in Iraq.

Zarqawi always remained committed to targeting the Jordanian government as he despised the crown and its pro-Western sympathies. Jordanian officials thwarted an AQI planned attack against the headquarters of the Jordanian Intelligence Services in 2004.[108] However, Zarqawi, always a student of missteps, successfully planned and executed the Amman Hotel suicide bombings in the heart of Jordan one year later. He followed the Amman attacks with a rocket attack against U.S. Navy ships in port at Aqaba and the firing of rockets into Israel from Lebanon.[109] Al Qaeda in Iraq was slowly spreading its operational reach across other geographic regions.

Zarqawi's network also continued to escalate the scale and frequency of attacks inside Iraq against the Shia, U.S. interests, Iraqi government, Iraq Security forces, and civilian-filled Baghdad hotels.[110] Statistically, from 2004 to 2005 insurgent attacks increased 29 percent.[111] Car bombs increased 108 percent, suicide car bombs increased 209 percent, and suicide vest attacks increased 857 percent.[112] However, the majority of the newly increased attacks against Shia and

---

[108] Mary Anne Weaver "Inventing Al-Zarqawi," *The Atlantic Monthly* 298, no. 1 (Jul/Aug 2006): 98.

[109] U.S. United States Department of State, Office or the Coordinator for Counterterrorism, Country Reports on Terrorism 2006, open-file report, (Washington, DC, 2006), 270.

[110] Ibid., 270.

[111] Donald Reed, "On Killing Al-Zarqawi - Does the United States Policy Know Its Tools in the War On Terror?" *Homeland Security Affairs* 2, no. 3 (July 2006): page nr., https://www.hsaj.org (accessed November 21, 2012), 3.

[112] Ibid.

Sunni civilians indicated an increase in sectarian violence.[113] Al Qaeda in Iraq, in conjunction with the insurgency, was rapidly increasing operations.

Al Qaeda in Iraq continued attacks against Shia in 2006. However, Sunni support for Zarqawi began to dissipate in the shadow of what would be termed the Sunni Awakening. Zarqawi retaliated by executing Sunni tribal chiefs.[114] Zarqawi claimed the killings were justified as the chiefs were cooperating with the Coalition forces and the Iraqi government. The escalation of the civil war Zarqawi fought so hard to incite began to fade. Shia militias and death squads stood down at the behest of the Iraqi government as the Sunni Awakening spread across Anbar province. In March 2006, a complex Al Qaeda in Iraq plot against the Green Zone was thwarted indicating some AQI faithful were changing sides.[115] Coalition forces gained traction against Zarqawi's network and began to capture tier one and two leaders throughout April and May of 2006. Zarqawi was finally killed on June 7, 2006, by a U.S. airstrike on his safe house.

Zarqawi planned and executed distributed Al Qaeda in Iraq operations in accordance with Schneider's distributed operations characteristic. Zarqawi planned and executed attacks throughout the country of Iraq, neighboring Jordan, and as far as Israel. Each attack sought to incite unrest and strife in line with his desire to expel Western influence and forces and to incite a civil war. Though eventually defeated and killed, Zarqawi nearly succeeded in instigating a full-blown civil war that may have led to the attainment of the Al Qaeda central strategic aim and most certainly, Zarqawi's aim.

---

[113] Donald Reed, "On Killing Al-Zarqawi - Does the United States Policy Know Its Tools in the War On Terror?" *Homeland Security Affairs* 2, no. 3 (July 2006): page nr., https://www.hsaj.org (accessed November 21, 2012), 4.

[114] Sean McClure, "The Lost Caravan: The Rise and Fall of Al Qaeda in Iraq, 2003-2007" (master's thesis, Naval Postgraduate School, 2010), 76-77.

[115] Anthony Cordesman, Eric Brewer, and Sara Bjerg, *The Islamists and the "Zarqawi Factor,"* (Washington D.C.: Center for Strategic and International Studies, 2006), 22.

Supporting operations through continuous and distributed logistics

ADP 4.0, Sustainment, defines logistics as the "planning and executing of the movement and support of forces."[116] Logisticians mainly deal with the planning, provision, distribution and acquisition of materiel, facilities, and services.[117] Unlike Bin Laden, Zarqawi was not independently wealthy or formally educated in business. AQI had to acquire external financing and materiel in order to execute operations while avoiding detection. Zarqawi's funding streams flowed mainly from sympathetic Muslims, charities, kidnapping ransoms, and other criminal activities. Aligning with Bin Laden increased Al Qaeda in Iraq's revenue by opening funding streams from wealthy Saudi donors already loyal to Al Qaeda Central.[118] Zarqawi also maintained connections to support networks in Germany and Italy for fund raising and document forging support.[119] Zarqawi's financers were wealthy. Fizz al-Din Al-Majid, a known Iraqi-based Zarqawi financial supporter, controlled between and $2 and $7 billion of assets to include over $35 million in his personal bank account at the time of his arrest in December 2004.[120] Insurgent groups in Iraq, including AQI, were raising funds of over $200 million per year as of 2004.[121]

Revenue was important to maintain operations for the organization's distributed operational cells and immense payroll. Zarqawi's network employed bomb makers, media

---

[116] U.S. Department of the Army, ADP 4-0, *Sustainment* (Washington, DC, Government Printing Office, July 2012), 1.

[117] Ibid.

[118] Timothy Kraner, "Al Qaeda in Iraq: Demobilizing the Threat" (master's thesis, Naval Postgraduate School, 2005), 15.

[119] Jean-Charles Brisard with Damien Martinez, *Zarqawi: the New Face of Al-Qaeda* (New York: Other Press, 2005), 157-160,165-166.

[120] Anthony Cordesman, Eric Brewer, and Sara Bjerg, *The Islamists and the "Zarqawi Factor,"* (Washington D.C.: Center for Strategic and International Studies, 2006), 19.

[121] Peter Bergen, "Self-Fulfilling Prophecy," *Mother Jones*, NOV/DEC 2007, 89.

professionals, electricians, drivers, and suicide bombers. One electrician, AbulGamal, revealed to U.S. interrogators he was paid fifty dollars per job to wire hundreds of suicide vests and roadside bombs.[122] He denied making car bombs as well as moving the explosives implying a separate payroll requirement for vehicular bomb making and drivers.[123] Abu Bayda, Zarqawi's cell leader in Mosul and member of Al Qaeda's Mujahideen Shura Council, described how the organization acquired and trafficked weapons from Iran.[124] He also described the movement of suicide bombers and weapons through a network of safe houses.[125] Suicide bombers were housed, fed, and received religious support prior to executing attacks. A common practice also required payment of remittance to the families of bombers upon successful execution of an attack. Zarqawi also employed media programmers to edit and upload videos to websites. Ismail, a former college student in computer science, was recruited from a Mosque and offered a job to edit and upload videos to militant websites while maintaining anonymity.[126]

Manpower was critical to the sustainment of Al Qaeda in Iraq operations. Attrition of bombers through successful attacks as well as coalition interventions reduced the available AQI tactical manpower. Zarqawi maintained European contacts that possessed passports and remained steadfastly loyal to the AQI ideology of attacking Western targets.[127] Al Qaeda in Iraq drew in

---

[122] Matthew Alexander and John R. Bruning, *How to Break a Terrorist: the U.S. Interrogators Who Used Brains, Not Brutality, to Take Down the Deadliest Man in Iraq* (New York: St. Martin's Griffin, 2011), 132-134.

[123] Ibid.

[124] Ibid., 217.

[125] Ibid.

[126] Ibid., 196-197.

[127] Rod Nordland et al., "Fighting Zarqawi's Legacy," *Newsweek*, 6/19/2006, 32-35.

recruits from numerous countries to include Tunisia, Algeria, and Saudi Arabia.[128] Suicide bombers were not in short supply and Zarqawi effectively employed them. Numbers estimate Zarqawi's network was responsible for up to 90 percent of suicide attacks in Iraq at the height of the Insurgency.[129] Al Qaeda in Iraq is credited with recruiting and employing the first female European suicide bomber when in 2005; a Belgian couple detonated their suicide vests targeting a coalition convoy.[130]

Iraq also proved fertile ground for weapons and munitions. The dismantling of the Iraqi Army during the U.S. invasion left stockpiles of artillery and mortar shells unsecured. Former Iraqi soldiers who joined the insurgency provided the expertise in employment of mortars. Zarqawi's explosive experts were skilled in rigging devices from small suicide vests to large explosive laden vehicles or implanted IEDs. The sheer number and dispersion of Al Qaeda in Iraq linked attacks displays the strength of the organizations logistics and sustainment. The Iraqis within AQI assisted in insuring the logistics networks blended into the local environment.

Zarqawi's vast network of loyalists, sympathizers, and supporters enabled AQI to support operations through continuous logistics. Criminal activities and donors provided funding for supplies while sympathizers provided safe haven for lines of communication. Zarqawi's suicide bombers, his preferred attack medium, flowed freely into AQI. Zarqawi avoided large logistics storage sites and centralized stocks through continuous logistics flow to geographically distributed cells.

---

[128] Anthony Cordesman, Eric Brewer, and Sara Bjerg, *The Islamists and the "Zarqawi Factor,"* (Washington D.C.: Center for Strategic and International Studies, 2006), 17.

[129] Associated Press "Al-Qaeda Arranges Most Suicide Blasts in Iraq, U.S. Says," *Washington Post*, April 11, 2006.

[130] Peter Bergen, "Assessing the Fight Against al Qaeda", Testimony to the U.S. House Permanent Select Committee on Intelligence (April 9, 2008), 13.

Task organize into operationally durable formations

Al Qaeda in Iraq organized into operationally durable formations for both security and to widen influence. As previously stated, the durable formation is designed to conduct distributed operations over an indefinite period of time by dispersing combat power into self-contained combined arms formations.[131] The operationally durable formation also supports the planning and execution of simultaneous attacks against a distributed enemy. Zarqawi's organization of Al Qaeda in Iraq was designed to empower centralized target selection and decentralized detailed planning and execution of attacks. The estimated committed strength of AQI within Iraq ranged from 1500 to 5000 fighters dispersed throughout five major urban areas: Fallujah, Mosul, al-Qaim, al-Anbar, and Baghdad.[132] Al Qaeda in Iraq consisted of trained fighters from Afghanistan as well as Zarqawi's camps in Northern Iraq. His top tier lieutenants were his closest advisors who oversaw larger portions of the network such as operations, logistics, and media.[133] The second tier leadership was responsible for planning and resourcing operations within Iraq.[134] Resourcing included the flow of foreign fighters, bombers, money, information, and munitions.[135] The third tier of Al Qaeda in Iraq consists of local cells responsible for attack execution.[136]

---

[131] Schneider, James J., Vulcan's Anvil: The American Civil War and the Foundation of the Operational Art. Theoretical Paper No. 4 (Fort Leavenworth, KS: U.S. Army Command and General Staff College, 2004), 50.

[132] Youssef Aboul-Enein, "Abu Musab Al-Zarqawi an Examination of the Writings of Investigative Journalist Gamal Rahim," *Infantry Magazine* 98, no. 4 (August-December 2009): 15.

[133] Anthony Cordesman, Eric Brewer, and Sara Bjerg, *The Islamists and the "Zarqawi Factor,"* (Washington D.C.: Center for Strategic and International Studies, 2006), 4.

[134] Ibid.

[135] Ibid.

[136] Ibid.

The U.S. military credited Zarqawi's organization as responsible for more than 90 percent of suicide attacks in Iraq in April 2006.[137] Suicide bombings require an extensive network of explosive experts, transportation assets, reconnaissance, and coordinators. Rarely are suicide attacks the work of a single individual working alone. Zarqawi's organized cells demonstrated ability to execute geographically distributed attacks, sometime simultaneous, spanning international borders. The implications of the complexity of attacks indicated tactical cells internally possessed the required skill sets to resource and execute independent attacks. Each cell also consisted of a security element, local leadership, and was commanded by a regional emir, or a tier one AQI member.[138] Zarqawi insured the support of the network of cells through the creation and maintenance of centralized support to include scholars to issue fatwas, spiritual leaders for religious and ideological guidance, and media support for information operations.[139] Suicide bombers, demolition and ammunition support also filtered down through Zarqawi's logistics and financial networks.[140] Zarqawi's organization into distributed independent cells ensured the failure or destruction of a local cell would not destroy the entire network. Conversely, cells could continue to execute attacks if the leadership was decapitated as evidenced by the survival of AQI following Zarqawi's death. Overall, AQI was centrally controlled but organized

---

[137] Associated Press "Al-Qaeda Arranges Most Suicide Blasts in Iraq, U.S. Says," *Washington Post*, April 11, 2006.

[138] Anthony Cordesman, "Zarqawi's Death: Temporary "Victory" or Lasting Impact," (Washington D.C.: Center for Strategic and International Studies, 2008), 4.

[139] Randy Schliep, "A Time to Kill: When Is Leadership Targeting an Effective Counterterrorism Strategy" (master's thesis, Naval Postgraduate School, 2007), 73.

[140] Matthew Alexander and John R. Bruning, *How to Break a Terrorist: the U.S. Interrogators Who Used Brains, Not Brutality, to Take Down the Deadliest Man in Iraq* (New York: St. Martin's Griffin, 2011), 132-134.

into operationally durable formations capable of independent operations. Zarqawi's demise was ultimately the result of the infiltration of the central leadership circle.

Zarqawi organized AQI into operationally durable formations. AQI cells spanned Iraq and were capable of conducting independent operations under the operational guidance of Zarqawi or his trusted lieutenants. The size of the formations reduced the required footprint and enhanced the anonymity into the communities. The resiliency of the distributed durable formations enhanced AQI's survivability following successful attacks against cells by coalition forces.

Employ operational art against a distributed enemy

Zarqawi defined his enemies as the U.S., coalition forces, Shia Muslims, the government of Iraq, Iraqi security forces, and Western-influenced governments in the Middle East. He also maintained an especially strong hatred for the Jordanian government. He prioritized his efforts to focus initially on the closest targets, which were the Shia and the U.S. coalition forces. He engaged targets throughout the Sunni triangle and expanded throughout Iraq and adjacent countries. The U.S. and coalition forces were headquartered in Baghdad and spread throughout the country. In 2004, the U.S. forces in Iraq numbered around 138,000. The forces combined with coalition forces located on forward operating bases throughout Iraq and headquartered in Baghdad. Supply convoys maintained lines of communication from Kuwait and northward. The U.S. forces broke down portions of Iraq into battle spaces designated as multi-national divisions that were occupied and patrolled by division size elements. The division areas were subdivided into brigade level battle spaces. The majority of the Shia population resided Southeast of the Sunni triangle. Zarqawi targeted Shia, coalition, and Iraq security forces targets throughout the country displaying the ability of Al Qaeda in Iraq to effectively target and degrade a distributed enemy.

Zarqawi targeted a vast array of enemy elements. The enemy ranged from small Shia neighborhoods to the large coalition base cluster in the Baghdad Green Zone. Zarqawi successfully executed attacks against enemies distributed geographically throughout Iraq, neighboring Jordan and Israel.

Choosing to accept or decline battle

Zarqawi, as mentioned above, chose to not to engage the invading U.S. forces upon the Iraq invasion. He preserved the strength of his network, finances, logistics, and fighters. Zarqawi began the fight against coalition forces when he decided the time was right. Zarqawi's organization was decidedly offensively focused in operations. Zarqawi, or one of his tier one lieutenants, chose targets and the general timeframes to engage. Every attack Al Qaeda in Iraq conducted was executed under the guise of Zarqawi. When he or his operatives were compromised, they simply disappeared into the population instead of fighting a battle against a superior force. Through choosing when and where to execute offensive targets and maintaining an active defense through operational security and evasion, Zarqawi maintained the initiative and surprise in engagements. Coalition efforts captured or killed operatives as well as degraded local cells. However, Zarqawi as the central figure remained the decision maker on when and where to attack. Until the U.S. intelligence community broke into his inner circle, targets and methods were largely a mystery until the attack was underway or imminent.

Zarqawi fought on his terms. He engaged targets when he wanted and where he wanted. He refused to confront the superior U.S. and coalition military might head-on and chose instead to hide among the population and strike at will. Zarqawi's tactical advantage lied in his ability to accept or decline battle at will.

Attack against an enemy center of gravity

Clausewitz defined the center of gravity as "the hub of all power and movement, on which everything depends."[141] Western military planners consistently struggle with identifying and targeting enemy centers of gravity in campaigns and major operations upon which to direct the decisive effort. Ideally, destruction of the enemy army forces within a state on state conflict should destroy the enemy's physical means to continue to fight and thus bring about peace negotiations. According to Clausewitz, victory is achieved when the enemy's will to resist is broken and he no longer possesses the means to resist.[142] State-on-state conflicts entail armed forces colliding on the battlefield fighting under the banner of the state in order to achieve a political aim. The political aim is enabled through the accomplishment of military objectives attempting to collapse of the will of the opposing force to continue to resist. The opposition's will is one element joint doctrine defines as a possible strategic center of gravity.[143] Operational and tactical centers of gravity are nested within the strategic centers of gravity.[144] The centers of gravity are normally plural and may metamorphose when directly attacked requiring continuous reassessment. Ideally, war plans orchestrate tactical actions to accomplish objectives under operational campaign plans. The objectives of campaign plans combine to achieve the military objective leading to achievement of the military end state.[145]

---

[141] Carl von Clausewitz, *On War,* Indexed Edition, Reprint ed. (Princeton: Princeton University Press, 1989), 595-596.

[142] Ibid., 75.

[143] U.S. Department of Defense, JP 5-0, *Joint Operations Planning* (Washington, DC, Government Printing Office, 11 August 2011), III-22.

[144] Ibid.

[145] U.S. Department of the Army, ADRP 3-0, *Unified Land Operations* (Washington, DC, Government Printing Office, May 2012), 1-6.

U.S. Military Joint doctrine defines centers of gravity as "the source of power that provides moral or physical strength, freedom of action, or act of will."[146] The Joint definition expands on Clausewitz's definition by categorizing centers of gravity as moral or physical. Zarqawi, as a non-state actor, could not directly engage the U.S. and coalition military in a force-on-force conventional conflict with Al Qaeda in Iraq. He had to define an approach within his operational means in order to attain his strategic aim. Dr. Joe Strange explained the moral center of gravity as rooted in the will of the people.[147] Moral centers of gravity are people centric and reside either within the populous leader, the populous ruling elites, or the population as a whole.[148] The moral centers of gravity are harder to understand and target, yet remain important due to their strategic influence.[149] Furthermore, the moral centers of gravity may prove an ideal objective when the means do not exist to attack the physical center of gravity.

Dr. Strange and Colonel Iron authored a two-part paper outlining a method for center of gravity analysis utilized by military planners and taught to United States Marine Corps planners. Strange and Iron recommend conducting both a friendly and enemy center of gravity analysis in order to determine enemy critical vulnerabilities to target with friendly critical capabilities.[150] Strange and Iron completed a moral center of gravity analysis specifically focused

---

[146] U.S. Department of Defense, JP 1-02, *Department of Defense Dictionary of Military and Associated Terms* (Washington, DC, Government Printing Office, November 2010), 48.

[147] Joseph Strange and Richard Iron, "Centers of Gravity: What Clausewitz Really Meant," *Joint Force Quarterly* no. 35 (2004): 25-26.

[148] Ibid., 26.

[149] Ibid., 27.

[150] Joe Strange and Richard Iron, *Understanding Centers of Gravity and Critical Vulnerabilities Part 2 a Useful Tool to Understand and Analyze the Relationship between Centers of Gravity and Their Critical Vulnerabilities: The Cg-cc-cr-cv Construct,* in the Air War College, http://www.au.af.mil/au/awc/awcgate/usmc/cog2.pdf (accessed November 11, 2012) 16.

on conflict between Western Democracies and Middle Eastern Terrorist groups.[151] This model easily transcends to the struggle between Al Qaeda in Iraq and the United States and coalition military forces.

Specific to Al Qaeda in Iraq, Zarqawi had to determine the center of gravity to target to best achieve his aim. Zarqawi desired to establish the caliphate base in Iraq and then expand the caliphate throughout the Middle East. Zarqawi realized his only option was to violently expel the U.S. and coalition forces from Iraq leaving a vacuum of governance. Zarqawi saw the U.S. government as the strategic moral center of gravity. In order to attack the government, he had to identify critical vulnerabilities to exploit. Strange and Iron identified the U.S. center of gravity as the President of the United States.[152] The critical capability the president possessed in regards to the conflict against Middle Eastern Terrorist Groups is the ability to "lead a concerted and sustained campaign to defeat extremist Middle Eastern terror groups."[153] As previously stated, Zarqawi did not possess the means to defeat the U.S. military in a force-on-force campaign and certainly not the President of the United States. He therefore needed to exploit critical vulnerabilities. The U.S. critical vulnerabilities Zarqawi targeted were the loss of interest in a protracted conflict with few actionable gains and the reaction of the U.S. population to mass casualties i.e.. the will of the American population to sustain the casualties attendant to the prolonged struggle in Iraq.[154] Zarqawi also gained an advantage by capitalizing on the lack of

---

[151] Joe Strange and Richard Iron, *Understanding Centers of Gravity and Critical Vulnerabilities Part 2 a Useful Tool to Understand and Analyze the Relationship between Centers of Gravity and Their Critical Vulnerabilities: The Cg-cc-cr-cv Construct,* in the Air War College, http://www.au.af.mil/au/awc/awcgate/usmc/cog2.pdf (accessed November 11, 2012), 20-21.

[152] Ibid., 21.

[153] Ibid.

[154] Joe Strange and Richard Iron, *Understanding Centers of Gravity and Critical Vulnerabilities Part 2 a Useful Tool to Understand and Analyze the Relationship between Centers*

U.S. human intelligence assets infiltrated into Al Qaeda and insurgent networks in Iraq to provide operational security and enhance his fighters' freedom of movement.[155]

According to Strange and Iron, the Al Qaeda aligned groups' critical capability was to "force the withdrawal of the U.S. and coalition forces from the Middle East through persistent terrorist attacks against US targets, thereby creating the condition where extremist groups can topple moderate Middle East regimes."[156] In aligning with Al Qaeda, Zarqawi accepted the role of Al Qaeda's emir in Iraq. He had witnessed the mujahedeen force expel the Soviet military from Afghanistan through a protracted fight. Zarqawi set two aims for Al Qaeda in Iraq: to incite a civil war between the Sunni and Shia and to expel the U.S. and coalition forces from Iraq.[157] He viewed the aims as interdependent and targeted both simultaneously. The civil war would create an unstable Iraq in international eyes and in turn reduce the support of the U.S. and coalition populations. The infliction of casualties against U.S. soldiers and citizens also aimed to dissuade the U.S. populous support.[158] Zarqawi began a campaign of violence against the Shia population to incite civil unrest. The Shia militias were already feared in Sunni circles. Zarqawi sought to increase the Shia attacks through targeted attacks against Shia population centers that he hoped in turn would lead to the uprising of the Shia militias against the Sunnis.[159] He postulated the

---

of Gravity and Their Critical Vulnerabilities: The Cg-cc-cr-cv Construct, in the Air War College, http://www.au.af.mil/au/awc/awcgate/usmc/cog2.pdf (accessed November 11, 2012) 21.

[155] Ibid.

[156] Ibid., 20.

[157] George Michael, "The Legend and Legacy of Abu Musab Al-Zarqawi," *Defense Studies* 7, no. 3 (September 2007): 346.

[158] Timothy Kraner, "Al Qaeda in Iraq: Demobilizing the Threat" (master's thesis, Naval Postgraduate School, 2005), 44.

[159] George Michael, "The Legend and Legacy of Abu Musab Al-Zarqawi," *Defense Studies* 7, no. 3 (September 2007): 346.

resultant Shia-Sunni civil war would destabilize Iraq beyond coalition control just prior to the 2005 Iraqi elections. He released a statement to Sunni men explaining the Shia attacks and encouraging the Sunni to join.[160] He hoped the resultant civil war and mounting U.S. combat casualties would gradually dissuade the U.S. populous support. Zarqawi also employed high visibility attacks on Iraqi security forces in addition to the Internet postings of gruesome beheadings and Al Qaeda attacks. Zarqawi was successfully attacking the U.S. strategic moral center of gravity through the critical vulnerability of populous support at the critical juncture leading into the U.S. 2006 election cycle.

Zarqawi chose an indirect method to attack the U.S. center of gravity. Strange and Iron's center of gravity analysis highlight key vulnerabilities AQI exploited. Zarqawi executed attacks against the Iraqi population to incite a civil war. Zarqawi flooded the Internet with videos and messages highlighting gruesome attacks and executions. Zarqawi attempted to create a steady rate of U.S. combat casualties. He targeted the U.S. populous support for the Iraq war, a key U.S. vulnerability, with his brutal tactics and media operations, his strengths.

The preceding section examined AQI operations as orchestrated by Zarqawi using the derived characteristics of operational art for the irregular warfare practitioner. First, Zarqawi successfully employed distributed operations against the U.S., coalition forces, Iraqi government, Western-friendly governments, and the Iraqi population in an attempt to achieve his strategic aims. Second, he employed a system of distributed and continuous logistics support throughout the AQI organization. Third, Zarqawi task organized AQI into operationally durable formations or cells. Each cell was able to conduct independent operations unconstrained by logistics. The task organization also provided force protection of the organization through compartmentalization

---

[160] Raj Purohit and Golzar Kheiltash, "Law and Ethics: Indicting Zarqawi for Genocide," *Georgetown Journal of International Affairs* 7, no. 2 (Summer 2006): 92-93.

40

and small geographically dispersed footprints. Forth, Zarqawi conducted attacks against a distributed enemy. AQI's attacked U.S. and coalition formations across Iraq and outside the country borders. Fifth, Zarqawi maintained the choice of when and where to engage the enemy in an attack. Finally, Zarqawi chose an indirect method to attack the enemy center of gravity.

CONCLUSION

Zarqawi, as the leader of Al Qaeda in Iraq, executed operational art against U.S. and coalition forces in Iraq from 2004 to 2006. During this period, he planned and executed distributed attacks against U.S., coalition, Iraqi security forces, and Iraqi civilians in order to obtain two campaign objectives. His campaign objectives were to incite a civil war between the Shia and Sunni populations within Iraq and to eject U.S. forces from Iraq and Western influence from Muslim lands. Zarqawi's campaign objectives were designed to meet the strategic aim of establishing the caliphate within Iraq, which embedded within the strategic aim of Al Qaeda Central. Zarqawi, an irregular warrior leading a regional terrorist organization, managed to spread the influence of Al Qaeda internationally during his orchestration of operational art.

In light of the derived definition of operational art and the derived characteristics, Zarqawi did employ operational art against U.S. and coalition forces in Iraq from 2004 to 2006. This monograph employed a view of an irregular warfare practitioner planning and executing operations against a superior state force, a method identified in the Cultural Perception Framework model.[161] Operational art, as executed by an irregular warrior such as Zarqawi, brings several implications to the future of military operations. First, it brings about more in depth understanding of the actions of the tacticians to the aims of the leaders. By viewing the U.S. forces through the eyes of Zarqawi, a unique perspective of U.S. vulnerabilities and critical

---

[161] *Red Team Handbook: Version 6* (Fort Leavenworth, Kansas: University of Foreign Military and Cultural Studies, April 2012), 145.

capabilities emerges. The vulnerabilities receive increased focus for protection while the capabilities are employed against the enemy vulnerabilities. Secondly, it assists in understanding an irregular enemy's approach whose strategic and operational aims are ideologically based. When viewing Zarqawi's tactical actions as nested under his operational aims, the disjointed attacks against civilians, U.S. and coalition forces, and Iraqi security forces appear more deliberate than random. Finally, violent extremists and non-state actors continue to create havoc in the international environment and threaten the United States and its interests, the U.S. will continue to maintain offensive actions against these networks.[162] Understanding that extremist actors engage in irregular warfare against the U.S. assists military planners in identifying terrorist network centers of gravity to direct U.S. power against.

Operational art has continued to mature from Schneider's Civil War battlefields to the irregular warfare domains in Iraq, Afghanistan, and Africa. In light of the military dominance of the U.S., non-state actors and state-sponsored terrorists will continue to engage the U.S. through irregular warfare methods. This monograph presented the case of Al Qaeda in Iraq employing operational art, in a hybrid form, in the irregular warfare domain, against a superior military force. Al Qaeda in Iraq, enabled through other participating insurgent entities, approached achieving its strategic aim. When viewed through an operational art lens, the question of how disjointed and geographically dispersed attacks threatened a superior military force and a dominant superpower becomes clear. Zarqawi, as an operational artist, fell short in applying his Sfumato to create a masterpiece.

---

[162] U.S. United States Department of Defense, Office of the Secretary of Defense, *Sustaining U.S. Global Leadership: Priorities for 21st Century Defense, open-file report,* (Washington, DC, 2012), 1.

BIBLIOGRAPHY

Primary Sources

Alexander, Matthew, and John Bruning. *How to Break a Terrorist: the U.S. Interrogators Who Used Brains, Not Brutality, to Take Down the Deadliest Man in Iraq*. New York: Free Press, 2008.

Bergen, Peter. "Assessing the Fight Against al Qaeda." *Testimony to the U.S. House Permanent Select Committee on Intelligence* (April 9, 2008).

Department of Defense. *Joint Publication (JP) 1-02, Department of Defense Dictionary of Military and Associated Terms*. Washington, DC: Government Printing Office, 2010.

Department of Defense. *Joint Publication (JP) 3-0, Joint Operations*. Washington, DC: Government Printing Office, 2011.

Department of Defense. *Joint Publication (JP) 5-0, Joint Operation Planning*. Washington, DC: Government Printing Office, 2011.

Department of the Army. *Army Doctrine Reference Publication (ADRP) 3-0, Unified Land Operations*. Washington, DC: Government Printing Office, 2012.

Department of the Army. *Field Manual (FM) 3-24.2, Tactics in Counterinsurgency*. Washington, DC: Government Printing Office, 2009.

Department of the Army: *Army Doctrine Publication (ADP) 4-0, Sustainment*. Washington, DC: Government Printing Office, 2012

Mir, Hamid. "Pakistan Interviews Usama Bin Laden". Islamabad, Pakistan (18 March, 1997).

Powell, Colin. "A Policy of Evasion and Deception: Full Text of U.S. Secretary of State Colin Powell's Speech to the United Nations On Iraq." Washington Post Online. http://www.washingtonpost.com/wp-srv/nation/transcripts/powelltext_020503.html (accessed February 7, 2013).

Red Team Handbook: Version 6. Fort Leavenworth, Kansas: University of Foreign Military and Cultural Studies, April 2012.

The Combatting Terrorism Center at West Point. www.ctc.usma.edu.

U.S. Department of Defense. Office of the Secretary of Defense. *Sustaining U.S. Global Leadership: Priorities for 21st Century Defense*. Open-file report. Washington, DC, 2012.

U.S. Department of State. Office of the Coordinator for Counterterrorism. *Country Reports on Terrorism 2005*. Open-file report. Washington, DC, 2006.

U.S. Department of State. Office of the Coordinator for Counterterrorism. *Country Reports on Terrorism 2006*. Open-file report. Washington, DC, 2007.

Secondary Sources

Aboul-Enein, Youssef. "Abu Musab Al-Zarqawi an Examination of the Writings of Investigative Journalist Gamal Rahim." *Infantry Magazine* 98, no. 4 (August-December 2009): 12-15.

Alberts, Sheldon. "Bush Warns Against Culture of 'defeatism': War On Terror, Iran Top List in Annual Address," *Ottawa Citizen* (1 February 2006).

Associated Press. "Al-Zarqawi Purportedly Releases Propaganda Video", *USA Today*(7/1/2005).

Associated Press. "Al-Qaeda Arranges Most Suicide Blasts in Iraq, U.S. Says," *Washington Post* (April 11, 2006).

Bell, Tom. "The Making of a Killer: Radical Islam Helped Turn a Two-Bit Thug Into Terrorist Commanding Global Attention," *Salina Journal*, (15 June 2006).

Bergen, Peter, and Paul Cruickshank. "Self-Fulfilling Prophecy." *Mother Jones* 32, no. 6 (Nov/Dec 2007): 48-49, 88-89.

Bergen, Perter. *The Osama Bin Laden I Know: an Oral History of Al Qaeda's Leader*, New York: Free Press, 2006.

Berman, Paul. "The Philosopher of Islamic Terror." *New York Times Magazine*, March 23, 2003.

Biddle, Stephen. "Seeing Baghdad, Thinking Saigon." *Foreign Affairs Journal* 85, no. 2 (March/April 2006): 2-14.

Clausewitz, Carl von. *On War, Indexed Edition*. Reprint ed. Princeton: Princeton University Press, 1989.

Cordesman, Anthony, Brewer, Eric, and Bjerg, Sara. "The Islamists and the Zarqawi Factor." *Center for Strategic and International Studies* (2006).

Cordesman, Anthony. "Zarqawi's Death: Temporary Victory or Lasting Impact." *Center for Strategic and International Studies* (2006).

DeYoung, Karen. "Bin Laden Lauds Al-Zarqawi On Tape / Iraq Al Qaeda Leader, Killed in Bombing, Called 'lion of Jihad'" *Washington Post* (June 30, 2006).

Farrall, Leah. "How Al Qaeda Works: What the Organization's Subsidiaries Say About Its Strength." *Foreign Affairs Journal* 90, no. 2 (Mar/April 2011): 128-38.

Gaddis, John Lewis. *The Landscape of History: How Historians Map the Past*. New York: Oxford University Press, USA, 2004.

Gerges, Fawaz A. *The Far Enemy: Why Jihad Went Global*. 2 ed. Cambridge: Cambridge University Press, 2009.

Knickmeyer, Ellen and Finer, Jonathan. "Insurgents Assert Control Over Town Near Syrian Border," *Washington Post* (September 6, 2005).

Kraner, Timothy. "Al Qaeda in Iraq: Demobilizing the Threat." Master's thesis, Naval Postgraduate School, 2005.

Martinez, Jean-Charles Brisard with Damien. *Zarqawi: the New Face of Al-Qaeda*. New York: Other Press, 2005.

McClure, Sean. "The Lost Caravan: The Rise and Fall of Al Qaeda in Iraq, 2003-2007." Master's thesis, Naval Postgraduate School, 2010.

Michael, George. "The Legend and Legacy of Abu Musab Al-Zarqawi." *Defense Studies* 7, no. 3 (November 2007): 338-57.

Nagourney, Adam. "With Election Driven by Iraq, Voters Want New Approach," *New York Times* (November 2, 2006).

Napoleoni, Loretta. "Profile of a Killer." *Foreign Policy* 151 (Nov/Dec 2005): 36-43.

Nordland, Rod, and Michael Hirsh. "Fighting Zarqawi's Legacy." *Newsweek* 147, no. 26 (June 19, 2006): 32-35.

Purohit, Raj, and Golzar Kheiltash. "Law and Ethics: Indicting Zarqawi for Genocide." *Georgetown Journal of International Affairs* 7, no. 2 (Summer 2006): 91-99.

Reed, Donald. "On Killing Al-Zarqawi - Does the United States Policy Know Its Tools in the War On Terror?" *Homeland Security Affairs* 2, no. 3 (July 2006): page nr. https://www.hsaj.org (accessed November 21, 2012).

Salhini, Claude. "Method of Zarqawi Madness," *Washington Times* (30 January 2005).

Schliep, Randy. "A Time to Kill: When Is Leadership Targeting an Effective Counterterrorism Strategy." Master's thesis, Naval Postgraduate School, 2007.

Schmitt, Eric. "Jet Plot Shows Growing Ability of Qaeda Affiliates," *New York Times* (December 31, 2009).

Schneider, James, J. *Vulcan's Anvil: The American Civil War and the Foundation of the Operational Art*. Fort Leavenworth, KS: U.S. Army Command and General Staff College, 2004.

Shaffer, Donald. "Unraveling Al Qaeda's Strategy." Master's thesis, Joint Advanced Warfighting School, 2005.

Smith, Craig. "At Least 23 Die in 2 Terrorist Bombings in Algeria," *New York Times* (April 11, 2007).

Stout, Mark, Jessica Huckabey, and John Schindler. The Terrorist Perspectives Project: Strategic and Operational Views of Al Qaeda and Associated Movements. Annapolis, MD: Naval Institute Press, 2008.

Strange, Joseph, and Richard Iron. "Centers of Gravity: What Clausewitz Really Meant." *Joint Force Quarterly* 35 (2004): 20-27.

Strange, Joseph, and Richard Iron. "Understanding Centers of Gravity and Critical Vulnerabilities Part 2 a Useful Tool to Understand and Analyze the Relationship between Centers of Gravity and Their Critical Vulnerabilities: The Cg-cc-cr-cv Construct." *The Air War College*: page nr. http://www.au.af.mil/au/awc/awcgate/usmc/cog2.pdf (accessed November 11, 2012).

Swain, Richard. Filling the Void: The Operational Art and the U.S. Army, in The Operational Art: Developments in the Theories of War, ed. B.J.C. McKercher and Michael A. Hennessey. Westport, Connecticut: Praeger, 1996.

U.S. Congress. U.S. Congressional Research Service. *Al Qaeda: Profile and Threat Assessment*, by Kenneth Katzman. CRS Report for Congress, Federation of American Scientists. Washington, DC, 2005.

U.S. Congress. U.S. Congressional Research Service. *Al Qaeda: Statements and Evolving Ideology*, by Christopher M. Blanchard. CRS Report for Congress, Congressional Research Service. Washington, DC, 2005.

U.S. Congress. U.S. Congressional Research Service. *Iraq and Al Qaeda*, by Kenneth Katzman. CRS Report for Congress, Congressional Research Service. Washington, DC, 2007.

Weaver, Mary Anne. "Inventing Al-Zarqawi." *The Atlantic Monthly* 298, no. 1 (Jul/Aug 2006): 87-88, 90-96, 98-100.

Weisman, Steven. "Threats and Responses: Security Council; Powell, in U.n. Speech, Presents Case to Show Iraq Has Not Disarmed," *New York Times* (February 6, 2003).

Whitlock, Craig. "The New Al-Qaeda Central," *Washington Post* (September 9, 2007).